Old America

50 stress relieving designs

by

Jack Baici

COPYRIGHT NOTICE

INTRODUCTION

This book contains 50 stress relieving designs obtained from Puck covers found in the Library of Congress.
Puck was the first successful humor magazine of colorful cartoons, caricatures and political satire.
It was published in the United States from 1871 until 1918.

Going through the rapids

An important factor

The age of prosperity

During the investigation

Little Ted Fauntleroy

When the iceman gets there

CORPORATION MAGNATE
REP. CAMPAIGN FUNDS
DEM. CAMPAIGN FUNDS
Kepler

Henceforth

July the fourth

TARIFF
REVISION
SPECIAL

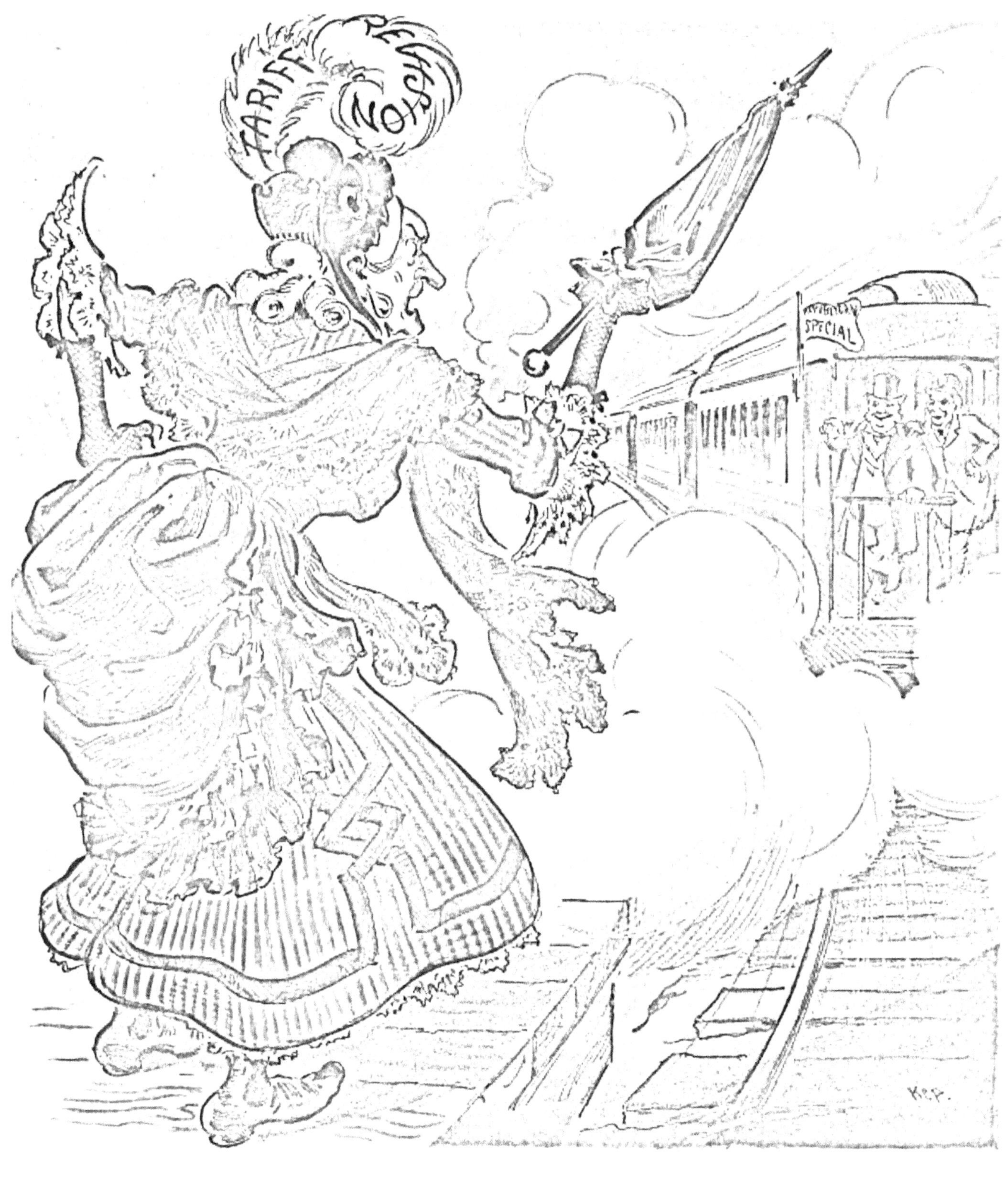

Left again

"I wander if I am his Valentine"

Never too late to run

Overworked

The gentlemen from New York

TARIFF LEGISLATION
TAXPAYER
U. S. SENATE
Keppler.

McKinleysm

Shoulder to shoulder

Old woman and old man

She has seen better days

The dear creatures

A natural inference

Our sleeping beauty

The new journalism beats him

The finishing touch

A dismal outlook

As the law stands

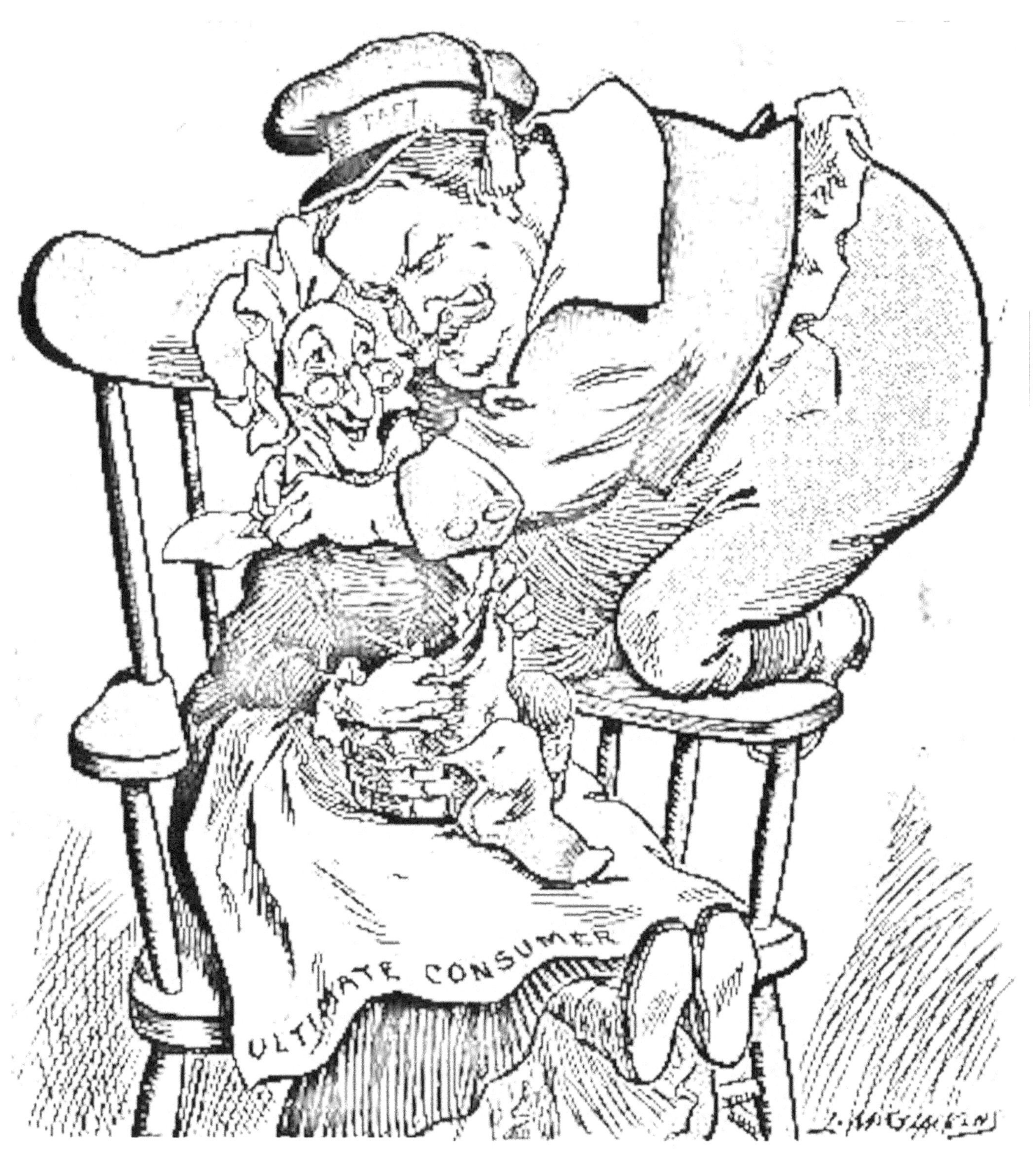

"I'll take care of you grandma"

The physician of the period

Hallo happy workers!

Dull

Back from Bololand

Discharged as cured

The political peanut vendor

Waiting for the balloon ascension

The gospel according to "St John"

What show have you got, little man?

The new baby

It may help some if Wall Street gave trading stamps

Two things he can't stop on Sunday

Conservatism

The endless search

The song of freedom

Willing to compromise

Uncle Sam's summer girl

He is learning better

Three happy old friends

Wrapped up in his pet idea

Puck's inventions

The biggest people on the road

The czar out for a job

The latest suitor

The national knife-grinder